EMPATH

Practical Guide for Dealing with Relationships, Narcissists, Energy Vampires, and Psychopaths

By Ashley Jones

© Copyright 2017 by _____ - All rights reserved.

The following eBook is reproduced below with the goal of providing information that is as accurate and as reliable as possible. Regardless, purchasing this eBook can be seen as consent to the fact that both the publisher and the author of this book are in no way experts on the topics discussed within, and that any recommendations or suggestions made herein are for entertainment purposes only. Professionals should be consulted as needed before undertaking any of the action endorsed herein.

This declaration is deemed fair and valid by both the American Bar Association and the Committee of Publishers Association and is legally binding throughout the United States.

Furthermore, the transmission, duplication or reproduction of any of the following work, including precise information, will be considered an illegal act, irrespective whether it is done electronically or in print. The legality extends to creating a secondary or tertiary copy of the work or a recorded copy and is only allowed with express written consent of the Publisher. All additional rights are reserved.

The information in the following pages is broadly considered to be a truthful and accurate account of facts, and as such any inattention, use or misuse of the information in question by the reader will render any resulting actions solely under their purview. There are no scenarios in which the publisher or the original author of this work can be in any fashion deemed liable for any hardship or damages that may befall them after undertaking information described herein.

Additionally, the information found on the following pages is intended for informational purposes only and should thus be considered, universal. As befitting its nature, the information presented is without assurance regarding its continued validity or interim quality. Trademarks that mentioned are done without written consent and can in no way be considered an endorsement from the trademark holder.

Table of Contents

INTRODUCTION — 1

CHAPTER 1: CHALLENGES AND SOLUTIONS OF THE EMPATH — 4

CHAPTER 2: HANDLING DIFFERENT RELATIONSHIPS AS AN EMPATH — 11

CHAPTER 3: DEALING WITH NARCISSISTS — 17

CHAPTER 4: HANDLING ENERGY VAMPIRES AND PSYCHOPATHS — 26

CHAPTER 5: GROUNDING AND COPING TECHNIQUES — 34

CHAPTER 6: THE HEALTHY RELATIONSHIP MODEL FOR AN EMPATH — 60

CHAPTER 7: THE EFT TECHNIQUE FOR HANDLING STRESS — 65

CONCLUSION — 76

OTHER BOOKS BY ASHLEY JONES: — 76

Introduction

Congratulations on downloading your personal copy of *Empath: Practical Guide for Dealing with Relationships, Narcissists, Energy Vampires, and Psychopaths*. Thank you for doing so.

Being a sensitive empath is a wonderful strength and asset. But this strength comes at a cost. As an empath, you are especially susceptible to emotional contamination, soaking up the emotions of others the way you would catch the flu, and being deeply moved by things beyond your control. But that's not all. Empaths may suffer from chronic stress, intense anxiety, physical illnesses, and pain more than the average person. In addition to this, the average empath requires plenty of recharge time after large social events or interactions. They require time to recover after a stressful day at work or after a holiday party.

Perhaps most difficult of all, being an empath can feel lonely, as if no one understands you. In extreme cases, you might feel like an alien or as though you are damaged in some way. This book was created with the intention of helping you solve this issue and navigate relationships and problematic people with ease and poise.

Do these Apply to you?

If you aren't 100 percent sure about whether or not you need help with areas, look to this checklist to find out.

You have a hard time setting boundaries:

It can be difficult for you to know when to say no to others or where to set boundaries because your moods and emotions get so entangled with theirs.

You aren't often present physically:

Empaths spend a great deal of time feeling the emotions of others, leading them to dissociate from their own bodies and experiences.

You soak up others' moods regularly:

You pick up on the moods of the people around you and even catch yourself feeling them hours later, in some cases. This can be friends or total strangers.

You have intimacy fears or issues:

You have a pattern in relationships where you get overly attached and close to someone and then go through painful separations from them. It always seems to be extremes when it comes to personal relationships.

Even once you start noticing them, these habits can be difficult to change because we have wired them into our brains. For this reason, and much more, to function healthily as an empath will require dedication and practice on a daily basis. Read on to find the answers you've been seeking.

There are plenty of books on this subject on the market, thanks again for choosing this one! Every effort was made to ensure it is full of as much useful information as possible. Please enjoy!

Chapter 1: Challenges and Solutions of the Empath

Envision exploring the earth, having interactions with other people, while being able to see into their hearts and feel their emotions. This is the normal path of a highly empathetic person (also known as an empath). This type of person is sensitive to others and can sense what they are feeling. There are some key qualities of strong empathy that begin when we're children and make it hard to transition into relationships once we begin dating.

These qualities include self-worth, knowing how to decipher true feelings from false, being introverted, and pleasing others. As empaths grow, they tend to build up methods for protection to block some of the emotional overflow bombarding them from every angle. When empaths don't understand their own patterns, these tendencies can manifest as addictions, bad habits, and other self-destructive actions. It can be overwhelming to sense so much, especially when it's feelings from someone you're romantically involved with.

This subject is so vast and complex, and we are only scratching the surface here, so let's start with the basics of navigating your romantic partnership or relation. Keep in mind that most of these tips can also help with other relations with co-worker, family, or friends.

Learning to release Emotions that aren't yours:

Recognizing your own emotions and learning how to care for yourself can be two very hard things to do when you're a natural empath. Empaths are constantly considering the feelings of others and forget to care for themselves. This is the first big mistake you can make when involved in any kind of relationship.

Recognizing the difference:

When you feel very strongly for someone and are connected to them, especially in a romantic sense, it's easy to sense their emotions. When you learn how to recognize whether they are your emotions or not, you'll immediately sense when something is amiss. Perhaps your loved one had a hard time at work, leading you to sense some kind of unbalance and feel confused. This simple situation can make you feel crazy, attempting to fix things in your life that don't necessarily need fixing.´

Taking time to reflect:

When you feel something like this, such as a mood that hits seemingly out of nowhere, pause and get calm. Then ask the universe to release the feelings you have inside of you that aren't yours. This will free you up to sit on your own with your own feelings for a while. Very quickly, you should notice a difference, helping you work with the emotions and leading you to feel calmer and more balanced. Once you're centered, you can support your loved one more authentically because you will be operating from your personal emotions and feelings instead of being muddied up by theirs.

Social Challenges and How to deal with them:

Socializing, when you're an empath, can be a challenge. Many people with this personality time have a difficult time with crowds, dates, or even smaller gatherings with family members. You might enter a restaurant full of people on an ordinary evening and find yourself suddenly feeling overwhelmed and sick, leading you to wonder whether you are picking up other people's feelings, have the flu, or something else entirely. It can be confusing and overwhelming at times. Situations like this could lead you to fear that you overreacted or made a fool of yourself.

It's more likely than not that eventually, you will be stuck in some situation that leads you to feel overwhelmed by what you're feeling. Here are some guidelines for helping navigate these difficult times:

Give yourself permission to leave or take a break:

When you feel uncomfortable with a situation, it's perfectly okay to take a break and be alone for a little while. In fact, this is a crucial aspect of living as a healthy empath. In some cases, you might even need the whole day to recover. Keep in mind that dating or having a partner could put you into new social situations that are more stressful than others.

When you can't leave:

There will, sometimes, be situations that you don't have a choice but to withstand. During these times, repeat to yourself that you're okay and that everything is okay. Say this over and over until you feel better. Depending on who you're with at the time, whether it's a partner or a friend, you could confide in them about what you're feeling. At times, just their reassurance can be enough to help you get calm and centered again.

The Importance of a Good Morning Ritual:

Grounding and protection are important for keeping yourself healthy as an empath. You need to have a morning ritual that helps you stay conscious of the feelings you will be picking up throughout the day. Each morning, take at least 15 minutes to ground yourself and think protective thoughts about your emotions and energy. This simple practice will improve your days and give you more space to work through the emotions you'll pick up while being around other people during the day. There isn't any one right way to do this. What matters more is finding what makes you feel most calm and centered.

Fitting into the empath category will impact your daily life in every way, regardless of whether you are in a relationship or not. For this reason, having the right spiritual tools in your repertoire will present you with a distinct advantage. As with all other gifts and talents, it requires time to find the techniques that work best for you. In the next chapter, we will discuss specific relationship challenges and methods for dealing with them and maintaining your own dignity and mental health.

Chapter 2: Handling Different Relationships as an Empath

One very common event that empaths experience is the back and forth effect that occurs when a person you're close to is having an intense emotion. Perhaps they are going through a hard time and choose to shut down, keeping you out of their personal space. Even when their state of mind isn't about you personally, it can lead you to soak up their depression, loneliness, frustration, or sadness. You may even mistake these feelings for your own and search for a reason for their existence, rather than realizing that they're coming from your partner. The effect becomes even more challenging when your partner is also an empath and you trade emotions back and forth. This can lead to confusion, helplessness, or feeling as though you're on the brink of insanity.

Taking it Slow in Romantic Partnerships:

Empaths are quite intense people. We know when we've found "the one" and can get carried away. When you've met the right person, you might be tempted to plan out your whole lives together within the first month of dating. Always remember to stay patient as you remain faithful to your personal feelings. After spending so much time overwhelmed by the emotions of others, feeling some of your own that are very strong can make you feel high on love. This will change constantly as fear comes in, leading to a rollercoaster of emotions if you aren't careful.

The importance of remembering to breathe:

In order to stay on top of this rollercoaster and make sure it doesn't carry you away into destruction, always remember to breathe before anything else. Living in the moment, connected to your breath and body is the best thing you can do as a highly emotional and perceptive person. We all fall victim to overanalyzing at times, especially empaths, but try your best to allow your relationship to unfold naturally and live in the now. Enjoy your time together and try not to rush too much.

Have some trust that it will all work out:

Try to trust that life is always working out exactly as it should and doesn't need to be rushed by you. If you're inclined to do so, you can pray to help keep you centered. Otherwise, simply think of other times that everything aligned in perfect timing and trust that the same will happen with the current relationship you find yourself in.

Disengage from the Emotional Intensity:

The absolute best thing you can do in the situation listed above is to disengage from the situation temporarily and get centered. When you do this, the other person can benefit from your calm state of mind, finding it easier to ground themselves. It takes a huge amount of awareness to remember to do this, but it will help you both shift to happiness and peace.

When you're in a romantic relationship with someone, you must know how to handle your own feelings and remain grounded, even when the interactions with your partner get intense. As the relationship deepens and grows, this skill will become even more important. Spending time with the other person on a daily basis and merging lifestyles and family members can be triggers for your emotions. Having proven and effective tools for dealing with these triggers will keep you balanced and grounded, even in the most trying of times.

Triggers from past relationships:

As an empath in a romantic partnership, you might find that past issues arise that lead you to feel panicked and fearful. You might be tempted to avoid the relationship or end it, even when you deeply care for the person, which is a very difficult impulse to deal with in the correct way. Everyone has their triggers and these triggers can leave you jumping from partner to partner, even when that's not what you mean to do. In many cases, you might not even recognize that you're carrying around a trigger until a brand new relationship begins.

You may have a trigger that is based on communication troubles in relationships. You might have had a past relationship with a person that lied to you and kept information from you on purpose to cheat or manipulate. Then you may meet a wonderful person who seems to be a great match for you, but notice a couple months into it that they seem to be acting secretive. Due to your past with a similar situation and emotion, your fears and ego will instantly believe that the same scenario is unfolding. There are many possible reasons why a person could be acting secretive that have nothing to do with cheating. Maybe they are having family troubles or working with their own trigger.

Handing these triggers in a healthy way:

The healthiest and smartest way you can recognize these signs and deal with them before they get to a breaking point is by being honest about the way you feel. This is, of course, a challenge since you will be putting yourself out on the line and making yourself vulnerable. On top of this, both knowing what you feel and knowing how to describe it can be challenging. There are a few things you should do before asking your partner for a talk. Firstly, ensure that your own energy is safe and protected and that you feel grounded and centered. Otherwise, the talk won't go as well as it could.

Go with your intuition:

In addition, if you have a feeling that one of these talks is necessary, ask your intuition to guide you in finding the perfect time to have it. Then remain open and receptive to any answers that may come through so you will know, in your gut, when you should have the conversation. As an empath, you have extremely heightened senses and intuition, so use this to your advantage to steer you in the right direction. It's important not to have this conversation when you or your partner are frustrated, angry, or tired. Of course, you should also remember not to give into the temptation to blame your partner if the situation gets tense.

Never try to make your partner feel bad for how they feel.

Be vulnerable and open with your partner:

Keep in mind that conversations are all about give and take. If you want your partner to tell you the truth, you should meet them on even ground and share vulnerable things about yourself, as well. That will keep the communication lines open between both of you. Go with your gut, notice when the timing is right and introduce topics as you see fit. Remember that the best way to have a relationship is to give it your all.

Chapter 3: Dealing with Narcissists

Interactions and relationships with narcissists are some of the most painful and dangerous experiences possible. These can range from surface level interactions to actual relationships that involve regular emotional and mental interactions. When you're involved with a narcissist, it's only a matter of time before exploitation and manipulation follow. Empaths are generous, kind people who feel the emotions and needs of others on a deep level. Why, then, would an empath get involved with a narcissist?

The empath:

Although it sounds hard to imagine to some, empaths actually get entangled with this personality type disproportionately often. This is because empaths are nurturing and sensitive, and when this isn't taken with caution, it can be harmful to their own wellbeing. They will almost always put other people's needs before theirs before they learn healthier habits, which is one major reason they are so attractive to the narcissistic personality type.

The narcissist:

Narcissistic personality types are morally and emotionally bankrupt, selfish people who cannot feel empathy in a meaningful or true way. They will never think about the feelings of other people and might not even stop to realize that others do have feelings at all. They always talk about themselves, are often huge braggers, and seem cruel and uncaring about the people around them. These traits may not shine through immediately, however, since narcissists are good at appearing charming. But if you pay close attention, small signals will show even during the very first meeting.

The result:

It might not seem like these two personality types would be drawn to each other, but it does happen quite frequently. As an empath, it's something you need to watch out for. Or perhaps you've already been sucked into a relationship with a narcissist and need to know how to heal from it or prevent the same thing from happening in the future. On the surface, it's obvious why the narcissistic type would feel attraction for an empath. They embody everything a narcissist doesn't; kindness, support, emotional awareness.

Warning Signs of a Narcissist:

A narcissist will always envy that which they don't have and will find any way to try to possess them, or even ruin the traits so that others can't have them. They will talk down about others, play up their own traits in a very arrogant way, and boast endlessly. To unsuspecting people, this may appear to be true confidence, but to the adept observer, it's obviously a front. You must learn how to recognize these signals so you can turn and walk away whenever you encounter a narcissist. But if you're already entangled with a narcissist, don't worry, you can free yourself.

Since the empath is so free and open about his or herself, they are a very attractive target for the narcissistic personality type. The narcissist will sense an emotional wellspring that they can leech from, taking and taking as the empath continues to give. All relationships between the narcissist and the empath will take this shape. What is it about the narcissist that appeals to the empath? At first, it's the strong vibe that the narcissist radiates, catching the empath's attention and impressing them. They might even have a degree of emotional intensity that the empath finds irresistible.

The dangers of getting Involved:

The narcissist is often hard to figure out emotionally, and for the empath who almost always has an easy time figuring people out, this is an appealing challenge. For this reason, the empath will be drawn to the narcissist, wanting to figure them out. Unfortunately, the more someone deals with a narcissist, the likelier they are to get hurt or even crushed. The narcissist will review endless abuse and endless reasons as to why he or she is wonderful. Can an empath really fall for this? Unfortunately, yes, but only when he or she is not aware of the dangers and signs of the narcissist. Here are some tips for that:

Pay attention when something feels wrong:

The empath's ability to read people doesn't go completely out the window when an appealing narcissist enters the picture. In fact, the empath will typically notice that there's something wrong or off about the person very soon. However, something stronger often overrides this, such as the narcissist's emotional needs. You, as the empath, may feel an irresistible draw to help them. But more often than not, the narcissist is putting on a show. In other cases, they really are wounded but cannot be helped. This is what causes the appeal, you as an empath want to help the narcissist but never can.

Realize that you cannot help them:

Although the narcissist will often fool an empath into thinking that they can be helped, this is not the case. Although the empath thrives on believing that they are helping the narcissist, it's often at the cost of your own peace of mind. By believing these lies, you are feeding the issue and letting the narcissist win your attention. This leads to codependency and further manipulation. This can be prevented entirely if you just recognize that a narcissist can never be helped by anyone but his or herself.

Cut off contact with them:

An empath can lock themselves into a situation where they are stuck caring for a perpetual victim who has no desire to get better and only seeks attention. Once you recognize the patterns of the narcissist, you can avoid this and cut off contact with them immediately. Although it's hard, delete their phone number, block their social profiles, and don't talk to them anymore. Most narcissists are harmed by their psychological disorder and cannot function in normal relationships except for in superficial ways. If you're not careful, as an empath, you may get sucked into taking care of someone indefinitely, always hoping you can fix them.

Watch out for the manipulation:

The specifics of a narcissist's manipulation may vary, but it will essentially look the same. Fortunately, you can avoid it if you watch for these signs:

- The narcissist claiming they will be lost without you.

- Him or her pulling the victim card and not claiming responsibility.

- The narcissist twisting reality and making the empath doubt everything.

It may be true that none of this is their fault, but it's also not yours and you shouldn't submit to punishment for mistakes made by someone else. If you maintain the relationship with a narcissistic person, that's what will happen. It may be painful to "abandon" someone who appears to need help, but looking out for oneself should be primary.

Take responsibility for your part:

The blame doesn't lie entirely on the narcissist in the situation where an empath gets entangled with them. You, as the empath, have to be responsible for the part you played in encouraging or enabling the narcissistic person. Perhaps, at one time, they even fulfilled your needs romantically or as a close friend. This can be true even if the relation was mostly painful or harmful. Without taking this important step, you are at risk for repeating this same pattern in other relationships and still being drawn to narcissists.

In Summary:

One can never expect a narcissistic person to recognize their own problems. This means it's up to you to recognize what's happening and either prevent it from progressing into something destructive, or remove yourself from the life of the narcissist as soon as possible. The most important realization you can have is that getting out of the situation should be your top priority. The narcissist is never going to change and is not capable of the empathy needed for healthy relationships.

Chapter 4: Handling Energy Vampires and Psychopaths

Energy vampires are people who feed off of drama, cause problems on purpose, lie for no apparent reason, make threats, and manipulate others by any means possible. All of us have known at least one person like this in our lifetimes. These types are usually not ill-intentioned (at least not consciously), but are instead victimized by their own nature and mind. They might feel paranoid and powerless, seeking out addictions and distraction from their misery in any way possible.

Energy vampires are not aware of the fact that they are the ones creating their lives and reality. Instead, they are always thinking about what they lack and don't think that getting love is possible for them. As a result, they think they need to take what they need from those around them and empaths make an especially attractive target to them due to their giving and caring nature. The empath wants to give them attention and care because they can see that the person is hurting, but attention to this drama is the fuel that keeps them going.

Energy vampires have no Wish to be Saved or Healed:

An energy vampire is all about survival. And when they have an endless source of "food" or energy to feed off of (your empathy), they won't have any incentive to fix their own issues or heal in any meaningful way. But interactions with these types are not without their own purpose. Here are a few things you can learn from them:

They can tell you about your level of self-love:

An energy vampire doesn't come into your life by accident. They can only do so if the door is open, and you open that door by doubting yourself. You might crave approval or be dealing with your powerless feelings. A habit toward co-dependency is the most attractive target an energy vampire can see. You might only feel okay with life and about yourself when you can help people. You might also feel as though you don't deserve love until you've earned it or feel guilty for having happiness when others do not.

You can only attract what you already are:

You might be addicted to the energy vampire type due to the drama they bring to your life. Perhaps you thrive on being needed and find satisfaction in the energy vampire's path of destruction. The fact of the matter is that you can only attract what you already are yourself. Your beliefs and thoughts create your personality and draw others to you.

Actionable Steps for Fending off Energy Vampires:

Thankfully, you can start taking steps right now to ensure that you stop attracting this type into your life and even solve the problems within you that keep drawing them to you.

Focus on having a high vibration:

Prioritize that in life which makes you happy and fulfilled. This will heighten your vibration to such a degree that an energy vampire will not be drawn to you due to how differently you two think. Set healthy boundaries, make time to care for yourself, and prioritize your own peace of mind.

Feel good as often as you can:

What energizes you and makes you feel better than anything else? This is what you should be prioritizing in your life. When you love yourself and enjoy life on a regular basis, those who bring you down won't want to be around you.

Be more like who you want to attract:

The best way to attract the people you want is to embody the characteristics you want to draw to yourself! If you hope to have well-adjusted, competent, respectful friends around you, you first need to protect these traits. Identify the beliefs that are holding you back and replace them with something more empowering and positive.

Know your Self-Worth as an Empath:

Empaths will always have a hard time with self-worth at least once in their lives. Their struggle to attaining it can have an impact on their relationships, leading them to sacrifice their true selves in favor of keeping someone around who doesn't like those true qualities. Feeling as though you aren't good enough for your loved one is a terrible feeling that makes you want to hide. It's possible to get so invested in a relationship that you lose who you are on a deeper level. Another way to prevent yourself from being victimized by energy vampires and narcissists is to encompass and embrace your true self, at all times.

Dealing with Psychopaths:

Psychopaths are not capable of feeling empathy the same way the rest of us can and can be dangerous to get involved with, especially for empaths. Here is some advice for handling them in your life:

Understand that some individuals just aren't good to be around:

Maybe you think that every person out there has a little bit of good in them or can be helped. The first and most crucial realization you can have is that some people really don't have a conscience. No matter how pure your intentions are, you cannot change this. All you can do is get to know your own weaknesses better before they are exploited by someone like this.

Watch their actions instead of their words:

Psychopaths will have endless lies, rationalizations, and excuses. For this reason, you shouldn't listen to their words but instead, watch what they actually do. How are you to tell when someone made an honest mistake from when they are being intentionally manipulative? Go for the rule of three strikes. If someone has told one small lie or broken a single promise, it could be an honest mistake. When you're at three lies, you're dealing with someone who acts without a conscience.

Build up your relationships and reputation:

If you are in a situation where you are forced to work with a psychopath or share a social circle with them, make sure you are building up your own relationships and reputation to prevent them from spreading misinformation about you. Work your hardest, keep your word, and work on having great relationships with your boss and co-workers. When you're handling a psychopath in your friend group, listen to warnings people give you about a certain person, especially if they come from multiple sources.

Making the right agreements:

Psychopaths thrive on winning. If you have a way to make it seem more appealing for them to work *with* you, rather than against you, you might free yourself from becoming one of their targets. Of course, this should always be done with a healthy level of protection around yourself and only if you are in a situation where you have no choice but to interact with the psychopath on a regular basis.

How to become Emotionally Immune to these Types:

Empaths will get taken advantage of by psychopaths and energy vampires. This is an especially high risk when the empath is feeling overburdened, depressed, and anxious already from emotional overload. Similar to your physical body and nervous system, your immune and emotional systems have a hard time with boundaries. They can't tell what is coming from you and what's coming from the outside world. That leads you extra vulnerable to energy vampires and psychopaths.

You can practice hygiene, not for your body, but for your emotional and mental shield. Pay attention to the way you feel any time you spend time around other people. You will soon realize which individuals are harming your emotional and mental health and limit how often you spend time around them. Psychopaths will have an especially harmful impact on this, of course, and you should avoid them at all costs. When that isn't possible, just follow the guidelines given to you above. You never deserve to be victimized by someone like that, and it's crucial to keep that in mind at all times.

Chapter 5: Grounding and Coping Techniques

Having a highly empathetic nature can be emotionally (and even physically) exhausting. A lot of people don't even realize they have this personality type and have no idea how to wield their abilities in a healthy way. Throughout this chapter, we will give you actionable tips and techniques for harnessing your empath power, keeping negative energy at bay, and maintaining emotional health for yourself.

The Importance of Following Grounding and Coping Techniques:

Some empaths have not fully understood their own power or how to use it correctly. See if any of the following apply to you:

- Do you spend a lot of time wondering which of your feelings are really yours and which you've picked up from somewhere else?

- Do the emotions you pick up on seem to linger longer in your consciousness than they do in other people?

- Do you find yourself constantly feeling tired because of how much of your own mental energy you donate to other people?

If you answered yes to all or any of these, then all of these grounding and coping techniques are especially important for you. You must prioritize healthy handling of your empathetic abilities and that requires making time in your life for grounding and centering.

Male Empaths:

A lot of people mistakenly assume that high empathy is more of a female characteristic, but male empaths exist, as well. Many male empaths get put down and ostracized for having these traits and might even hide them away. If you are a male empath, you're not alone! You deserve support just as much as anyone else. Make use of the tools and tactics in this chapter so you can find your inner peace in life.

One of the first tactics taught to empaths for helping them maintain their inner peace is the skill of developing a shield body around yourself. This bubble will protect you from harmful stimuli and overwhelming feelings from your eternal world. Empaths are sensitive and can easily pick up this harmful stimulus from other people, particularly when their shield isn't very strong. So, how can you create and strengthen this shield?

Envision the shield around your body:

Visualization is a very powerful tool. Picture the shield covering your body, radiating around you. It might show up as a specific color and some find gold or white to be especially effective. Figure out which color feels the most powerful for you and visualize it as a moving, flowing substance instead of solid or static. The idea is to form a shield around you, not hardened armor. The shield needs to have a flexible composition so that what you do need can slip by it, and what you don't will stay out. Make sure you do this visualization every morning.

A rooting and grounding visualization:

Whenever you feel like you've been lost in your head a little too much and wish to come back down to earth, you can do this visualization. Envision that you are sending out roots from your feet into the ground below you. Start to breathe and envision that this breath is coming into and out of the center of these roots. As you breathe in, take in the earth's energy, and when you breathe out, get rid of all that is holding you back and weighing you down, including all doubts and negativity.

Using positive affirmations in your daily life:

Another foolproof method for being mentally and emotionally healthy, as an empath, is using positive affirmations on a daily basis. There are no words for how effective this really is! This helps you think about your own wellbeing, be present in your life, and live in your own moods and energy rather than getting lost in the emotions of the people around you.

Another useful visualization for centering:

As soon as you have gotten used to doing your shield body exercise each morning, start imagining that your being has a spark in its center that stands for your purest essence. As you focus on this, also notice your thoughts, emotions, and all bodily sensations. Try this every time you are by yourself, then start practicing it in social situations. Practice switching between focusing on this spark and focusing on the people around you and do it until you can do this at will any time you want.

Define what healthy compassion is:

As an empath, it's extremely important that you don't take on the responsibilities of others as you empathize with them. People can become so accustomed to caring for others that they might feel obligated to do so, but the fact is that you aren't. Compassion is good, but without defining what healthy compassion is, you can't utilize this in a healthy way. While it's good to be very compassionate toward your fellow humans, you are never obligated to go beyond what is healthy for you. The struggle, for many empaths, lies in defining where that line exists. As soon as you do find out, defining boundaries will become much easier, leading to cleaner and clearer relationships.

You can start by identifying both your light and dark sides:

Since empaths are such kind and caring people, people might think that they are saintly or even perfect. You may get unintentionally attached to the idea of being seen as the "nice" one. This may keep you detached from your own shadow side and even sharing honest thoughts with others when they aren't nice to hear. But sugarcoating the truth doesn't help you or the other person. Get in touch with your shadow side and get comfortable with feeling and expressing negative emotions, too. Everyone needs this kind of release sometimes.

Clearing and smudging on a regular basis:

Even if you aren't having a hard time dealing with your special empath abilities, you can release yourself from the energy of other people by smudging yourself on a regular basis. This is done by lighting a bundle of Palo Santo or Sage. You can also just take a bath, shower, spend some time alone, or go out into nature to re-energize. You can also intentionally keep your home free of negative residual energies by opening up the windows and curtains at least once a day (even in the winter), and dusting on a regular basis.

Take a bath with essential oils:

One amazing method for clearing out any residual emotional difficulty hanging around is to take a bath with essential oils. This has to be a bath, not a shower and you can light candles to create a more peaceful environment. However, this isn't absolutely necessary. Run a bath with warm, comfortable water and drop a few drops of your favorite essential oil in there. Some great scents to use are clary sage, lavender, or cinnamon. You can also mix the oils as you see fit.

Make sure you won't be disturbed and can have some quiet time to yourself. Soak in the tub for at least 15 to 20 minutes and it will have a transformative effect on your mood. If you don't have any essential oils at home, that's perfectly okay, as well. You can take a bath with just water or use bath salts. Another option is putting some tea leaves into the bath.

Make sure you Always get Plenty of time Alone:

Empaths are usually quite intuitive, easily sensing and soaking up other people's energy and moods. This can lead them to feel overwhelmed in public or crowded areas, during social interaction, or even by certain sensations or smells. First, you must recognize that solitude is not just a preference for you, but a deep need that must be fulfilled for a healthy mind and heart. Recognize that you need space to recharge your batteries on a regular basis and that you don't have to feel guilty about it. Here are some steps you can take to make sure you're getting that:

Going outside:

Get yourself into nature, even if it only means a short walk through the park down the street. Being around natural scenery can have a profoundly transformative impact on your mood and energy levels, making life feel more bearable.

Reading a lot:

Books are profoundly transformative tools that you should make use of. Try to focus on reading inspiring or positive stories that will have a therapeutic impact on your mood.

Listening to positive music:

Instead of watching TV, try listening to some calming music that makes you happy, lighting some candles and providing a peaceful environment. Don't forget to turn your smartphone off to get the most benefits possible!

Tracking your Emotions as an Empath:

Connecting with other people is great and valuable, but connecting with your own emotions should be your first priority. In fact, you have to get in touch with your inner voice to make relationships have any meaning at all. Some empaths may find it helpful to use a journal to track their emotions, while some will find it helpful enough to remember to pause throughout the day and take stock of what's going on inside of them.

You can even set alarm reminders on your phone that alert you to look inside and take inventory of your thoughts and feelings. This will create a positive habit.

Practice correct breathing:

Nothing is quite as useful for controlling your state of mind as utilizing the breath in a conscious way. No matter what you are doing or where you are right now, pause whatever you are doing and breathe for five minutes. There is actually a correct, healthy way to breathe. Follow these guidelines:

1. Start by inhaling through the nose and into your belly as slow as you can. Place your hand over your stomach and make sure that as you breathe in, it's expanding instead of

your chest expanding.

2. You can then breathe out slowly, as steadily as possible. Envision that with each breath you take, you're bringing the baggage and chaos inside yourself out and getting rid of it.

Don't try to take this too far at first, since deep breathing is intense and can bring a lot of emotional difficulties to the surface that you weren't ready to face. Keep in mind that slow steps are best at first until you become used to it. Just a few breaths will be sufficient for beginners. Breathing this way will be a challenge at first, but will have a huge impact on keeping your mind calm.

How the Physical body Relates to your Highly Empathetic Nature:

Empathetic personality types have an above-average ability to unify with others and help in troubling times. For this reason, and more, they are great at being intuitive healing forces for others. They also have a strong personality that others will find attractive or even irresistible. Along with these qualities, however, there are some shadow aspects to be aware of and plan for.

This is what you should think about to stay emotionally and physically balanced.

It's no secret that empaths can have a hard time developing boundaries between themselves and others. They offer up too much support for the feelings of others and can forget to nurture themselves, at times. You may even constantly have an alert state of mind, looking for crisis or drama that you can help with. How can you solve this?

Developing your core and physical center:

We've talked a bit about grounding and centering on a mental and spiritual level, but did you know that forming effective boundaries goes beyond the spiritual? It isn't only about mental considerations, but also has to do with being strongly rooted in your physical body. Namely, your core (the torso, abs, and back). One way to strengthen this is to do basic core strengthening exercises, such as crunches or planks. Working on the core of your body will help you revive your energy when your stores are low and keep you protected from harmful energy.

Feel your body as your truest home:

Imagine a scenario where you have gone out of town for the weekend and didn't lock up your house before you left. Not only that, but in this scenario, you left your windows and doors open, allowing any intruder to sneak in. This is what being an unprotected and unaware empath really is. The more often you abandon your own home to meet other people, disregarding your space, the harder it will be to have a healthy and balanced home to return to.

First, acknowledge that your body is your truest home and the refuge that always waits for you. No matter how much you've neglected it or forgotten about it in the past, you can always return to it as long as you're alive. Practices like spending a lot of time alone, practicing yoga, and meditating on a regular basis, will help you build a solid home that you can return to at any time.

Taking Breaks from Social Media and the Internet:

As an empath, your internal environment can be compared to a satellite radio that picks up on countless channels every day. Your internal system is always surfing the channels, listening to the broadcasts of other people's emotions and inner states. This can include anything from your spouse's anger about work matters, your co-workers fears about her relationship, or your friend's joy and happiness. This can cause your nervous system to feel overwhelmed, sometimes more often than not, leading to chronic stress, depression, and severe anxiety. In addition to all of this, constant alerts from your smartphone signaling Facebook notifications and emails can add to the overload.

What to do about this problem:

The best prescription for the issue outlined above is to notice when your system is starting to feel overwhelmed. This could feel like something humming in the back of your mind, a quickened heartbeat, or just increased sensitivity emotionally. Taking breaks from social media on a regular basis will do a lot to restore your emotional balance and bring you back to the inner peace you know that you deserve. You can also turn your phone off as often as you can.

Get in Touch with your Community:

For the average empath, intimate matters rely on reciprocity and space. You may crave spiritual connections, emotional bonding, and physical intimacy at sometimes, and at others feel like all you need is space. Since you're so giving, it leaves you as an attractive victim for narcissistic and psychopathic people, as we discussed earlier. In addition to this, you might have a hard time receiving love and attention since you're so used to being the one giving others support. As a result, you might suffer from not getting enough emotional nourishment from the people in your life.

How can you solve this issue?

The solution to this issue is to get more involved with your community. In order to feel more connected to others in an emotional way, when you aren't feeling emotionally nourished, try getting closer to your town or an interest you support. This can mean volunteering at a local homeless shelter or voting on a cause that matters to you. This can provide you with the emotional fulfillment you crave without sacrificing your own peace of mind to achieve it.

The Filter of the Empath:

One potentially harmful aspect to being an empathetic personality type is having a membranous, thin skin which has intense reactions to invasions, whether they are real or imagined. This thin skin can be "allergic" to many things, including food, certain people, and social environments. Internally, the skin mimics the pattern of self-destruction and harm. That will leave our nerve endings open and exposed to rage, shame, and the grief that exists in the people around us and ourselves.

What can disturb the empath's thin skin:

A small comment from one of our friends, someone asking for help when we can't provide it, or just a creepy comment from a stranger at the mall can ruin our mood within just a few seconds. This causes an internal alarm to go off and leads to us labeling the person as either safe or dangerous. Many years ago, this ability to filter was needed for our basic survival as human beings. As we grow, though, it can become destructive. This is especially true if we doubt our own insights.

We may build up certain narratives around our experiences, repeating the stories we've crafted about the people who disturbed our thin skin. We might even seek out support from others and ask them to agree with us about our judgments about others.

When the thin becomes a hard shell:

It can be comforting to have this support behind us in our fears, but the actions we take can make this safety/danger filter harden into a thick shell. Our narratives are hardly ever based on just one encounter, and we reinforce them again and again as life progresses. This shell can protect you from harm, which is great, but it can also hold us back from experiencing true intimacy and our real, genuine selves. In other words, the defense becomes a detriment to our inner health.

Reevaluating our judgments:

At times, the hardest part occurs when the interpersonal interaction has already passed and our system gets restored back to its original balance. We may start to feel as though the comfort the narrative provided us with has evaporated or dissipated. The task here, then, is to return to our judgments and filter, look at the decisions we made, and reevaluate them. It's possible to look at different angles of the situation, adding some self-compassion to our hindsight. In some cases, we can even ask other people for their ideas.

Using them to grow as a person:

Eventually, we will be able to acknowledge where our personal biases blind us and hold us back. Then, we can adjust our settings to harbor less judgment and be open toward people. Once you do this, you have tools to grow and improve with. The challenge is that empaths will have difficulty changing their internal filters when they feel crucial for survival and general safety. In addition, adjusting these familiar settings will stretch your sensitive empath skin, which can be uncomfortable. This is where retreating into silence and alone time will be most helpful. These environments will promote a space for inner reflection, allowing us to get used to the new changes.

Your Irreversible Nature:

Many empaths resent who they are and would rather just get rid of their abilities. For this reason, some may numb themselves with any distraction available, relationships, television, or even drugs. It's important to accept that this is who you are and it cannot be changed. Therefore, it's more important than ever to introduce a balancing schedule to your life that will help you cope with your personality to come to see it as the gift it really is.

Committing to finding balance in your life:

This program is not temporary. Instead, it requires that you work at it every day and commit to it for life. Having your own daily balancing tools that you stick with faithfully will help you get to know yourself in all the most important of ways, improving emotional rejuvenation and deepening your life.

The importance of good influences:

As an empath, you need a trustworthy and meaningful community, your own tribe who accepts you for who you are. It gets tough and lonely sometimes, as you know, and you need somewhere to unwind and be understood. As soon as you have experienced this level of understanding and acceptance, the challenge becomes branching out from it into unfamiliar territory which will push us to keep growing.

Escaping the idea of perfectionism:

Some mistakenly believe that change is all about transcending your past flaws, leaving them behind to reach perfection. But real spiritual growth and emotional wellness involves accepting and working with our unique challenges. Being an empath brings the struggle of knowing you're different and finding ways to cope with that so you can excel at life, as everyone wants to do. Your reward for the hard work you put into this will lead you to a stronger perspective.

A moment will arrive when someone or something activates your trigger points, sending you into a nervous reaction. However, this time when that happens, you will recognize it and have the option to stop it in its tracks. Instead of getting lost in self-judgments, you will recognize the signals that you have been activated and triggered; trouble breathing, a higher heart rate, strong emotions. You will feel an instant pull to launch into the same old narrative. You might curse your nature as an empath and wish that you could be "normal". Then, you will suddenly remember what you've learned and take a deep breath, stepping back to reset yourself and following the new techniques you've learned here in this book.

In situations like these, you will notice how worthwhile your practices of self-care really have been. You will notice that you feel resistance, but find it easier to yield than before. You will have developed a solid foundation in yourself, finally believing and seeing the value you can add to this world.

The Importance of Discovering Balance as an Empath:

Existing in this world as an empath means learning to live with paradox and constant challenges. Is there a way to live a fulfilling life, exploring meaningful relationships with those around us, while also making time and space to stay true to yourself? Here are some important pursuits to focus on:

Growing your levels of patience:

How do you know when to shift your focus from the outside world to the quieter inner space? Realize now that patience is key because quite a few more years might go by before you reach the place you want to be. You may be older than you thought you would be when you finally blossom and reap the full benefits of the inner work and patience you've put into your personal growth. But when you take control over your sensitive nature, create boundaries in the physical realm, and work on our filters, we become stronger progressively. This makes it easier to find the social circles you truly deserve and belong to and flourish as a result.

When we flourish in that way, even more positive influences will be drawn to you. As an empath, you are deeply creative, grounded yet intuitive, resilient, and magnetic. Wielding these abilities with balance will bring you a life full of meaningful endeavor and happiness.

Chapter 6: The Healthy Relationship Model for an Empath

As an empath, relationships are quite a challenge. Since you are a highly sensitive person acutely tuned to emotions, you feel everything much stronger than those around you. This probably makes it obvious why relationships would be a challenge. Feeling strong emotions about everything can be overwhelming. And although some empaths take their nature as proof that they belong in singlehood indefinitely, relationships can be the ultimate source of growth on your life path, especially when they are with the right person.

Everyone has unique qualities and discovering the style of relationship you can truly thrive in is all part of the process of getting to know your genuine self on a deeper level. Let's begin with what people you should avoid getting involved in relationships with, due to your highly empathetic nature. We already covered some ground on these types of people, but let's go over it again in a little more detail, and some other relationship dynamics to be wary of.

Psychopaths, Sociopaths, and Narcissists:

These three types can be lumped together since attempting to form relationships with any of them will lead you to a similar result. Of course, these types always appear charming at first, because that's how they get their way. But as soon as you give them your full desire and attention, it gets messy. This can lead to true disaster when you are already sensitive, feel everything deeply, and struggle to understand what's happening. Remorse, guilt, and shame are all emotions that may become a frequent part of your life if you get involved with such a person, while your partner would likely feel little to nothing about your emotions.

Dating other highly empathetic types:

This is something that many lonely empaths have probably envisioned with longing. It seems like the perfect match, but you may want to try to avoid this. This relationship could end up very challenging, particularly when you stop to think about the power of emotions as this type of personality. This could potentially be a huge amount of energy and momentum building up as your relationship progresses, and relationships are already challenging to begin with, most often. Being with another empath can be intense as you pick up on each other's emotions, fueling anxiety and tension until it builds to an unbearable crescendo.

Dating a highly sensitive person:

Relationships can be challenging, which is no secret at all. However, all of your efforts could end up paying off if you find yourself someone that fits into the following category. The best personality type you can date, as an empath, is someone who is highly sensitive. Highly sensitive people can be similar to empaths in that they also pick up on the subtleties of other people's emotions and general situations. But they are different from empaths because their feelings are not *quite* as heavy and impactful.

The benefits of dating a highly sensitive person:

The average highly sensitive person is attuned to their feelings, just as an empath is. However, there is a key difference between a HSP and an empath. A HSP can typically create some distance between themselves and their feelings when they need to be there for their partner, which is a must for a healthy relationship to work. Another bonus to this arrangement is that you will have a person who can understand your heart the way others can't and relate to the fact that you feel so deeply.

Chapter 7: The EFT Technique for Handling Stress

Sometimes, all you want is some relief from your intense emotions. The EFT technique (emotional freedom technique) can be used to optimize mental and emotional health and balance. Emotional health is often taken for granted and overlooked, but it's essential for your healing and physical health. Even the most physically healthy person will not reach optimal physical conditions if they have emotional barriers blocking them from full progress.

What can EFT help you with?

EFT is simple, easy, and can provide you assistance with the following issues and areas:

- Releasing negative feelings.

- Reducing addictions to food.

- Eliminating or reducing pain.

- Achieving your goals.

Known as a type of acupressure (on a psychological level), EFT is based on similar energy meridians as the better-known acupuncture techniques that have been used for thousands of years. However, EFT doesn't involve any needles. Rather, this method uses simple tapping motions with the fingers, meant to induce kinetic energy to the chest and head as you consider your specific issue. This could be some type of pain, an addiction, or even a traumatic situation or event from the past. You then speak positive affirmations aloud at the same time.

The result of doing this at the same time can short circuit the blocked off emotions you're experiencing, restoring the balance of your body and mind. This frees up the energy in your body for healing on a physical level and promoting overall balance in your mind and spirit. This is especially important for highly sensitive, empathetic types who are always experiencing a wide array of often intense emotions and feelings. This can help you reset yourself and get back to balance.

Skepticism about EFT:

A lot of people are wary at first when they hear about EFT and the principles it uses. But the energy that our body uses is increasingly gaining more and more credit in the West world. Other people are taken aback at first, or even amused at, the affirmation and tapping methodology, which will be covered in this chapter. But EFT has a very high success rate and is spreading quickly. Medical professionals using EFT techniques are now prevalent in all parts of the world. This chapter will give you guidelines for where and how to tap, along with the correct affirmation processes to follow. Then you can begin using EFT right away to help yourself and others.

The tapping technique and locations:

A few main areas are important to learn about to correctly use EFT, the technique and the locations you should be tapping, along with the affirmations you should use. By following the instructions here, you will be able to treat any mental or emotional difficulties that arise on your empath journey. The main, basic sequence in EFT only takes a little while to learn (a few minutes). You may find it helpful to look up an instructional video on exact tapping points, but just by reading about them, you should have no troubles finding them.

Please note that although it's crucial to do the tapping in the right place, you don't have to worry yourself about being perfectly precise. Tapping your fingers on the general area is enough. If it turns out your results aren't exactly what you imagined or you have a problem that is especially traumatic, don't stop trying. Rather, think about reading more in-depth on the topic of EFT to learn more or even consulting a professional on the matter. Some therapists that are found online will even give free phone consultations.

Using your fingertips in the correct way:

Your first task in learning EFT is to realize that you're using your fingertips to do the tapping. Your fingertips have multiple acupuncture meridians, meaning that you're using both those and the meridians you're tapping when you do this. Most traditional methods for EFT ask you to use your middle and index fingers on just one hand, but this can be either hand. The majority of the points for tapping are on both sides of your body, so you can use either side and even switch sides while you tap. You could, for instance, tap under the right arm at first, then, later on, tap under your left eye.

Using more fingers:

This approach has been slightly modified that allows you to use all fingers and both hands, allowing them to relax gently and create a natural line with a slight curve. When you use more than just two fingers, you have access to a higher number of points of acupuncture. It also covers a larger area, reaching more than you would with just one or two fingers. But plenty of people reach success using the typical two finger, one-handed method. Use whatever appeals to you, but the modified version will be found, by some, to be a complete option.

Remove jewelry to prevent interference:

Take off your bracelets or watch so it won't interfere when you tap on your wrist. Ideally, you should be using the tips of the fingers instead of the pads of the fingers. The fingertips contain a higher number of meridian points. Please note that if you have very long nails, it will be more effective to use the pads of your fingers. You will also want to take off your glasses since they can electromagnetically and mechanically interfere with the process. If you are just doing a quick session at home by yourself, this isn't as important but still provides more convenience.

How to use EFT tapping methods:

Your taps should be solid, but never hard enough to bruise or hurt your skin in any way. In the event that you do use both of your hands for this, you can alternate the tapping motion. Make it so that each of your hands are tapping to a different beat instead of simultaneously tapping. This allows for a variant in kinesthetic and can add some extra benefits to the process. When you start tapping on the areas we will go over below, tap between five to seven times. The exact amount doesn't matter so much, but should line up with the amount of time a single, full breath requires.

The tapping points given to you will gradually make their way down your body. In other words, each point of tapping exists below the previous one. This makes it easier for you to memorize the movements and should only require a few repetitions before you completely commit it to memory for future use. But the sequence is not the most critical of all aspects to this. In fact, you are free to tap the different points in whichever order you prefer. Just make sure that you cover each point.

Can you use EFT in Public without Embarrassment?

A lot of people worry about using EFT in public places and getting embarrassed. These actions can call quite a bit of attention to you, especially when you use the revised version that includes more fingers and body parts. But after getting used to this technique on your own at home, you can switch to using just one hand and two fingers, and repeating your affirmation to yourself silently or very quietly. This will allow you to perform EFT techniques anytime, anywhere, without being embarrassed. In fact, the people around you will be unlikely to notice you're doing anything out of the ordinary.

Using tapping points:

The next step for using EFT is making sure you're using the correct areas for tapping, also known as tapping points. We will cover them in the order that you should be tapping them in, progressing down the list.

- The crown of your head, running your fingertips down the middle of your skull, back to back.

- The eyebrow, tapping to the side and above your nose where your eyebrow begins.

- The outer side of your eye, along the bone that borders your eye.

- Underneath your eye, tapping the bone that exists about an inch under the pupil.

- Under your nose, tapping the space between the lip and nose.

- The chin, tapping between the lower lip and the tip of your chin.

- The collar bone, tapping at the place where your first rib and collarbone join together. This point is highly important and can be found by placing your first finger on the notch that exists hear your breastbone (where a tie would be tied). At the bottom of this point, move the finger closer to the navel by a single inch and then move over one inch. This is the right place to be tapping and is called the collar bone in EFT even if it isn't strictly the collarbone.

- Underneath your arm, tapping at the point right in the center of your upper arm. This point would be aligned with your nipple if you are a male, and the center of your bra strap if you are a female. The point is four inches underneath the armpit.

- The inside of the wrists is the last tapping point for this exercise.

Again, the order you should tap in is the crown of the head, your eyebrow, the bone at the side of your outer eye, underneath your eye, underneath your nose, the center of the chin, your "collar bone," the center of the upper arm, and finally, the inside of your wrists.

Using affirmations with EFT Tapping:

Perhaps the most important aspect of all to the method of EFT tapping is using positive affirmations along with the tapping motions. Various versions of affirmations are talked about in self-help and motivational seminars. Positive affirmations are especially helpful for empaths, who often struggle with their personal worth and power. As you perform the tapping instructions listed above, you can say any of the following:

- "I know my own worth and know how to say no."

- "I prioritize my own happiness and know when to take a break."

- "I love myself and set healthy boundaries."

- "I wield my powers of empathy in healthy, responsible ways."

- "I am respected by the people around me."

- "I am attracting positive circumstances into my life every day."

- "I accept myself, no matter what challenges may come up."

- I am attracting only healthy relationships into my life."

A quality affirmation can shift your life in a specific, asked for direction. It's a statement of purpose and although it doesn't always reflect your current reality, it can call new conditions into existence, changing your life. Using them with EFT tapping is extra effective for the reasons stated during the beginning of this chapter. EFT taps into important energy challenges, freeing energy blocks and allowing you to rewrite your life story.

Remember to practice your affirmations:

Affirmations do require some time to work. Even though EFT does make them work faster, you will still need to work on it for a while before you see the results you want. Commit to doing this at least once a day for 20 minutes and you will begin to see changes within a month or two. If you keep repeating the affirmations you've chosen, they will become a reality.

Conclusion

Thanks again for downloading *Empath: Practical Guide for Dealing with Relationships, Narcissists, Energy Vampires, and Psychopaths*. You should now have a greater understanding of how to navigate relationships, deal with narcissists, and keep yourself centered even in the most trying of situations.

Always remember that staying grounded and centered and prioritizing your own inner peace will make everything else in life easier. Following these guidelines will ensure that your enhanced empathy is always a gift and not a curse.

If you enjoyed this book, please take the time to leave it a review on Amazon! Thank you and best of luck on your empath journey.

Other Books By Ashley Jones:

If you enjoyed reading this book then I recommend for you to check the following ones:

- **Empath: Practical Guide For A Life With A Special Gift - https://www.amazon.com/dp/B0727VRW59**

Made in the USA
San Bernardino, CA
04 December 2018